Fun with ROMAN NUMERALS

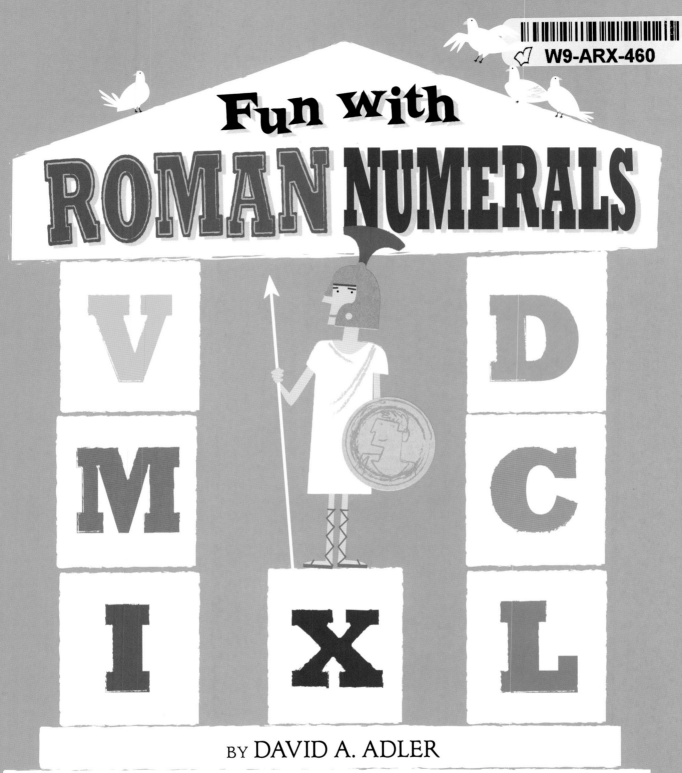

BY DAVID A. ADLER

ILLUSTRATED BY EDWARD MILLER III

Holiday House / New York

Write your age on a sheet of paper.

If you wrote

8, 9, 10, 11, or 12,

you wrote your age using

ARABIC
NUMERALS.

There's an older number system,

a very different number system,

that people still use:

ROMAN
NUMERALS.

If you write your age—
8, 9, 10, 11, or 12–
in Roman numerals,
you would write

**VIII
IX
X
XI
or
XII.**

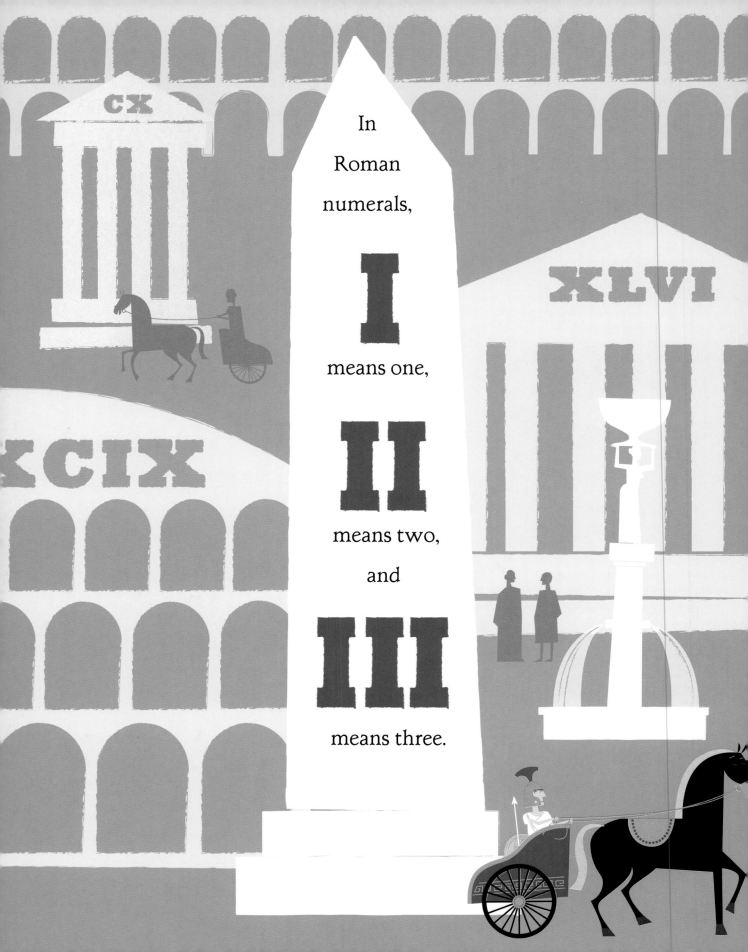

In Roman numerals,

I

means one,

II

means two,

and

III

means three.

In many modern books, Roman numerals are used to number some pages or to number the chapters. In a book that uses Roman numerals to number its chapters, Chapter **I** would be the first chapter. Chapter **V** would be the fifth chapter. In Roman numerals, **V** means 5.

The numbers on many watches and clocks are written in Roman numerals. If the hour and minute hands of a clock both point to **XII**, it's twelve o'clock. In Roman numerals, **X** means 10 and **XII** means 12.

Chapter V

Many sports events, including the football championship called the Super Bowl, are numbered using Roman numerals. Super Bowl **XLV** is the forty-fifth Super Bowl. In Roman numerals, **L** means 50, and **XLV** means 45.

There are ten digits in our number system:

1, 2, 3, 4, 5, 6, 7, 8, 9, and 0.

There are seven basic number symbols in Roman numerals:

I, **V**, **X**, **L**, **C**, **D**, and **M**.

In Roman numerals,

I	= 1	**C**	= 100
V	= 5	**D**	= 500
X	= 10	**M**	= 1,000
L	= 50		

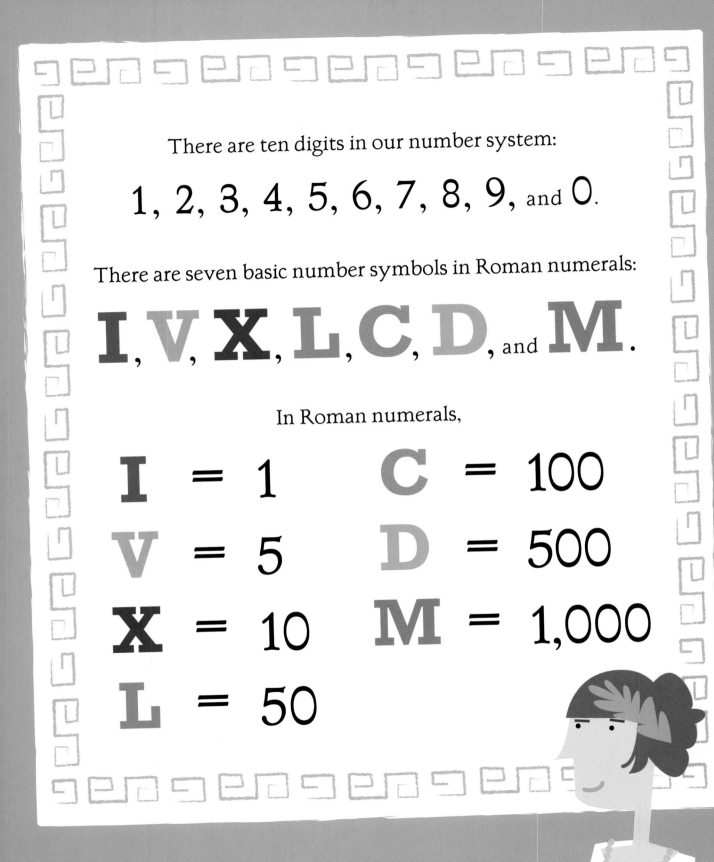

In Roman numerals, there is no symbol for zero.

In our system, the same numeral can have different meanings.

The numeral 2 by itself means two.

The numeral 2 in the number 26 means twenty.

The numeral 2 in the number 264 means two hundred.

Our system uses the position of numerals to show value. When the position of a numeral in our system changes, its value changes.

2

26

264

Roman numerals are used differently.

The value of a Roman numeral never changes.

I

1

V **always means** 5

X 10

Roman numerals use addition
and subtraction to write numbers.
In Roman numerals, when the same
numeral is repeated one after the other,
the numerals are added.

X means **10**

XX means **10 +**

XXX means **10**

C means **100**

CC means **100 + 10**

CCC means **100 + 1**

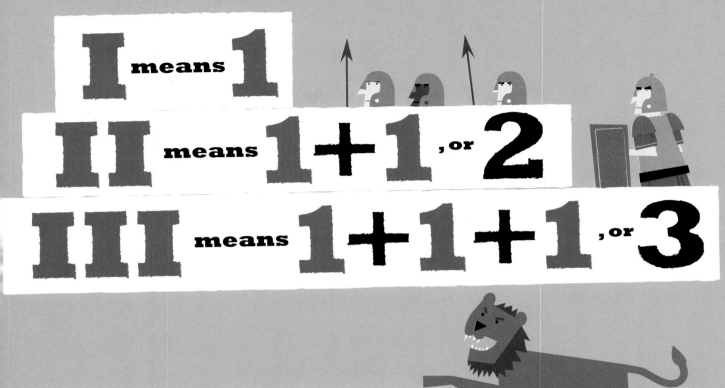

I means **1**

II means **1+1**, or **2**

III means **1+1+1**, or **3**

10, or **20**

+10 +10, or **30**

0, or **200**

00 +100, or **300**

In Roman numerals, when a larger numeral is followed by a smaller numeral, the numerals are added.

XVI means

X + **V** + **I**, or

10 + **5** + **1**,

or **16**.

In Roman numerals,

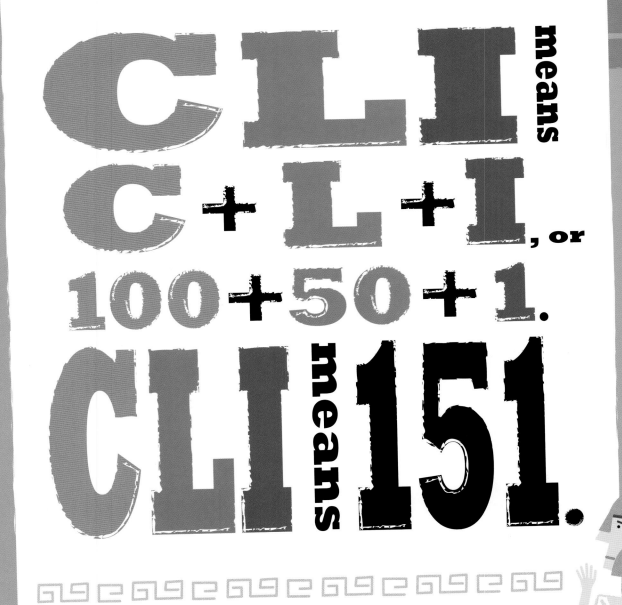

CLI means C + L + I, or 100 + 50 + 1.

CLI means 151.

In Roman numerals,

C + C + L + X + V + I + I, or

100 + 100 + 50 + 10 + 5 + 1 + 1

V I I I, or

means 2 6 7.

In Roman numerals, when a smaller numeral is followed by a larger numeral, the smaller is subtracted from the larger if the larger is no more than ten times the smaller.

In Roman numerals,

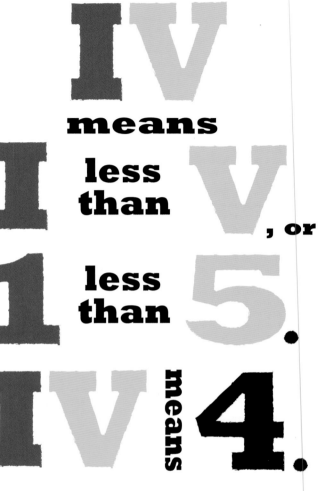

IV means I less than V, or 1 less than 5.

IV means 4.

It's easy to understand how this works if you think about buying something that costs four cents. You can pay a nickel (5¢) and get a penny (1¢) in change.

Apples
IV

VI   III

In Roman numerals,

IX means

I less than **X**, or

1 less than **10.**

IX means **9.**

It's easy to understand how this works if you think about buying something that costs nine cents. You can pay a dime (10¢) and get a penny (1¢) in change.

Pumpkins IX

IX   VII

In Roman numerals,

X **C** means

X less than **C**, or

10 less than **100**.

X C means

90.

It's easy to understand how this works if you think about buying something that costs ninety cents. You can pay a dollar (100¢) and get a dime (10¢) in change.

In Roman numerals,

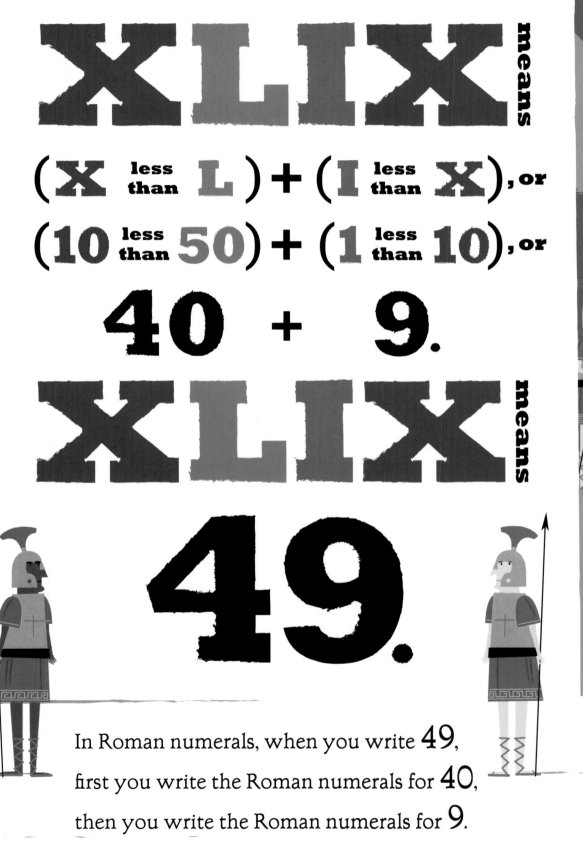

XLIX means

(X less than L) + (I less than X), or

(10 less than 50) + (1 less than 10), or

40 + 9.

XLIX means

49.

In Roman numerals, when you write 49,
first you write the Roman numerals for 40,
then you write the Roman numerals for 9.

XCIX means

$($ **X** less than **C** $)$ + $($ **I** less than **X** $)$, or

$($ **10** less than **100** $)$ + $($ **1** less than **10** $)$, or

90 + **9.**

XCIX means

99.

In Roman numerals, when you write 99, first you write the Roman numerals for 90, then you write the Roman numerals for 9.

CMXCIX means

(**C** less than **M**) + (**X** less than **C**) + (**I** less than **X**), or

(100 less than 1,000) + (10 less than 100) + (1 less than 10), or

900 + 90 + 9.

CMXCIX means

999.

In Roman numerals, when you write 999,

first you write the Roman numerals for 900.

Then you write the Roman numerals for 90.

Then you write the Roman numerals for 9.

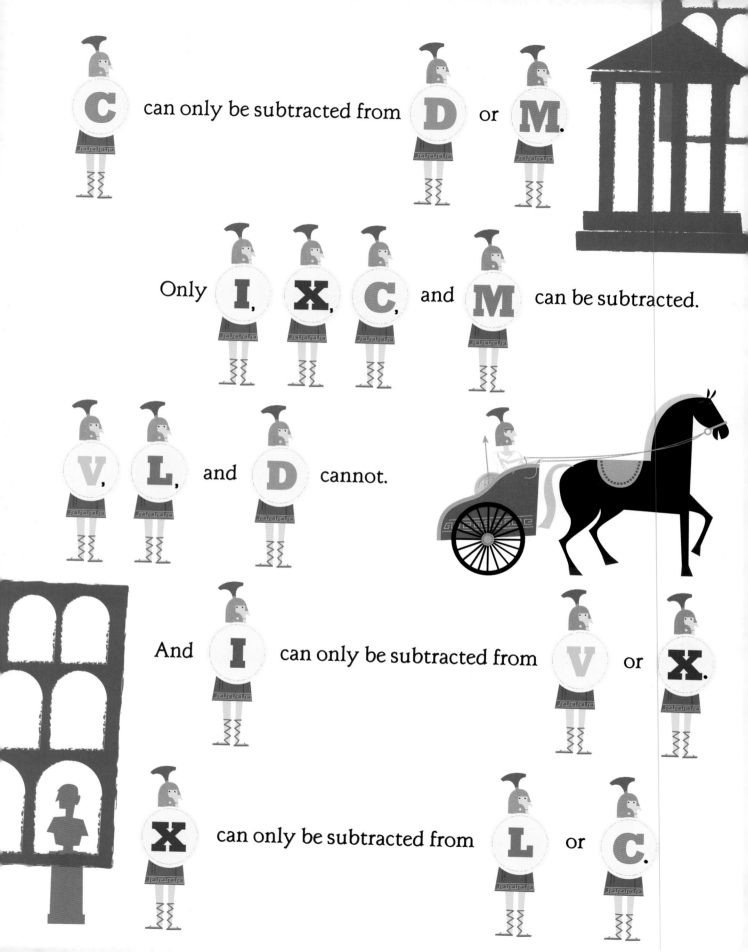

C can only be subtracted from **D** or **M**.

Only **I**, **X**, **C**, and **M** can be subtracted.

V, **L**, and **D** cannot.

And **I** can only be subtracted from **V** or **X**.

X can only be subtracted from **L** or **C**.

You can use coins to help you practice writing Roman numerals. Take three pennies, one nickel, three dimes, one half-dollar, three dollar coins, and some small blank sticky labels. Stick a label on one side of each coin. You will probably have to cut the labels so that they just cover the coin.

Write **I** on each of the penny labels.

Write **V** on the nickel label.

Write **X** on each of the dime labels.

Write **L** on the half-dollar label.

Write **C** on each of the dollar coin labels.

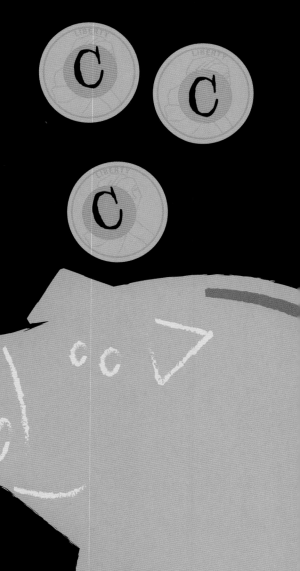

Do you know why you took just three pennies,

three dimes, and three dollar coins?

In Roman numerals, you don't need

more than three consecutive **I**s,

more than three consecutive **X**s,

or more than three consecutive **C**s.

You would not use four **I**s when writing 4.

You write 4 as **IV**.

Do you know why you took just one nickel

and just one half-dollar?

There is no Roman numeral with more

than one consecutive **V** or more than one consecutive **L**.

You would not use two **V**s to write 10.

You write 10 as **X**.

You would not use two **L**s to write 100.

You write 100 as **C**.

Lay the coins on the table with their label sides down. Select the coins that together are 26 cents. Now place them in the proper order to write 26 with Roman numerals.

Now turn the coins over so that you see the Roman numerals. Put the Roman numerals in the proper order to write 26.

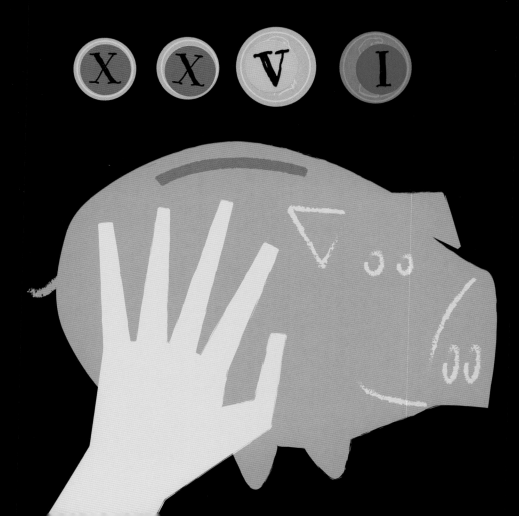

Select the coins you would use to make **24** cents.

You can't make **24** cents with the coins you have. You can make **25** cents and get **1** cent change. Select the coins to do that.

Have you noticed that you selected the same coins to write **24** as you selected to write **26**?

Now, put the Roman numerals in the proper order to write **24**.

Use the coins to help you write **38** in Roman numerals.

Use the coins to help you write **54, 59, 75, 106**, and **350**.

You can write 5,000 and other large numbers in Roman numerals. The bar on top means "thousand."

V̄ means 5,000

X̄ means 10,000

L̄ means 50,000

C̄ means 100,000

You can write even larger numbers in Roman numerals.

The open box means "hundred thousand."

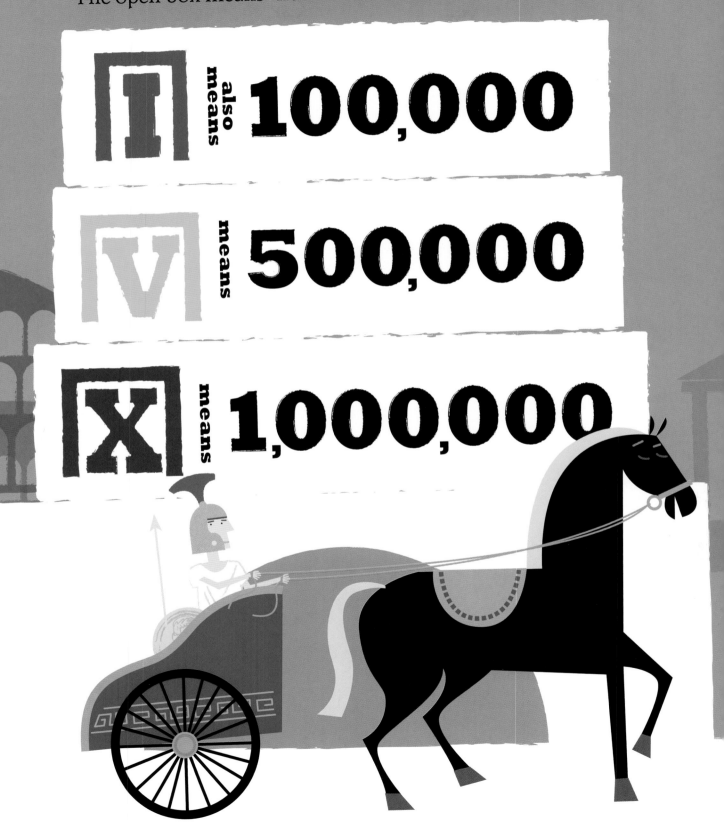

I — also means **100,000**

V — means **500,000**

X — means **1,000,000**

Be on the lookout for Roman numerals. Once you look for them, you may be surprised at how often you see them on clocks, in books, and on the sides of buildings. It's fun to read and write numbers in Roman numerals.

Chapter XVIII.

Mr. Frank Churchill did not come. When
posed drew near, Mrs. Weston's fears were
arrival of a letter of excuse. For the presen

With thanks to
Professor Stephen Krulik of
the Department of Curriculum,
Instruction, and Technology
in Education of Temple
University for his help.

Text copyright © 2008 by David A. Adler
Illustrations copyright © 2008 by Edward Miller III
All Rights Reserved
Printed and Bound in October 2016 at Tien Wah Press in Johor Bahru, Johor, Malaysia
The text typeface is Clemente Interro.
The illustrations were created on the computer.
www.holidayhouse.com

3 5 7 9 10 8 6 4

Library of Congress Cataloging-in-Publication Data
Adler, David A.
Fun with Roman numerals / by David A. Adler ;
illustrated by Edward Miller III. — 1st ed.
p. cm.
ISBN-13: 978-0-8234-2060-5 (hardcover)
ISBN-13: 978-0-8234-2255-5 (paperback)
1. Roman numerals—Juvenile literature.
I. Miller, Edward III, 1964-, ill. II. Title.
QA141.3.A339 2008
513.5—dc22
2007043531